NEW YEAR'S CUSTOMS AROUND THE WORLD

A GLOBAL TRADITIONS COLORING BOOK

HAPPY
New Year

PAMELA PETTYFEATHER

Copyright © 2025 Pamela Pettyfeather

All rights reserved.

No part of this book may be reproduced in any form or by any electronic or mechanical means, including information storage and retrieval systems, without written permission from the author, except for the use of brief quotations in a book review.

INTRODUCTION

Every culture has its own way of welcoming the New Year—and some of them are wonderfully strange. From grapes eaten at midnight to bells ringing 108 times, from bear costumes dancing through snowy streets to tin melted into secret shapes, people all around the world use symbols, foods, colors, and tiny rituals to invite a lucky year ahead.

Some traditions chase away bad spirits. Some welcome good fortune. Others wish for health, travel, prosperity, or simply a fresh start. But no matter where you are, the New Year is a moment of magic when we pause, look back, and imagine the twelve months to come.

This coloring book is a celebration of those moments. Inside, you'll find rituals old and new, silly and serious, cozy and bold. Each page invites you to color your way into the stories that shape New Year celebrations across the globe. Along the way, you might even discover a lucky tradition of your own.

So grab your pencils, open your imagination, and step into a world of sparkling superstitions, hopeful habits, and bright beginnings.

Here's to a colorful year—and to all the good luck you can carry!

Pamela

TABLE OF CONTENTS

RITUALS, SYMBOLS & MIDNIGHT MAGIC 7

FOODS & FLAVORS OF GOOD FORTUNE 41

NATURE, LIGHT & RENEWAL 63

PUZZLE: MATCH THE COUNTRY TO THE TRADITION! 73

ACTIVITY: 12 GRAPES, 12 MONTHS, 12 WISHES FOR THE NEW YEAR 75

HOW DO YOU SAY "HAPPY NEW YEAR" HERE? 83

MORE FROM PETTYFEATHER PUBLISHING 87

JOIN OUR MAILING LIST FOR BONUS PRINTABLES & FUN FACTS! 92

RITUALS, SYMBOLS & MIDNIGHT MAGIC

As the clock strikes midnight, people everywhere perform rituals meant to chase away misfortune and welcome bright beginnings. Some traditions are loud and dramatic—burning effigies, smashing plates, ringing bells—while others are quiet, symbolic, or delightfully strange. From fox masks to chimney sweeps to wishes burned over champagne, these customs remind us that humans have always used imagination and symbolism to mark the turning of the year. Here, you'll discover the stories behind the gestures that make New Year's Eve feel magical.

GERMANY
LUCKY LADYBUGS

In German folklore, ladybugs ("Glückskäfer," or "lucky beetles") are cherished symbols of protection and blessing. Farmers once believed that a ladybug landing on crops meant a healthy harvest, and a ladybug landing on a person meant the Virgin Mary had sent it to guard them. Over time, these spotted red beetles became beloved emblems of New Year luck, appearing on cards, candies, and decorations exchanged between friends and family.

Spotting a ladybug during winter—when they're usually hidden away—is considered especially fortunate. Because they eat pests and protect gardens, they're seen as tiny guardians of prosperity. At New Year, they represent fresh starts, gentle protection, and the hope that the months ahead will be fruitful and kind.

DID YOU KNOW?

The number of spots on a ladybug has inspired many superstitions—some say counting them predicts how many happy months lie ahead.

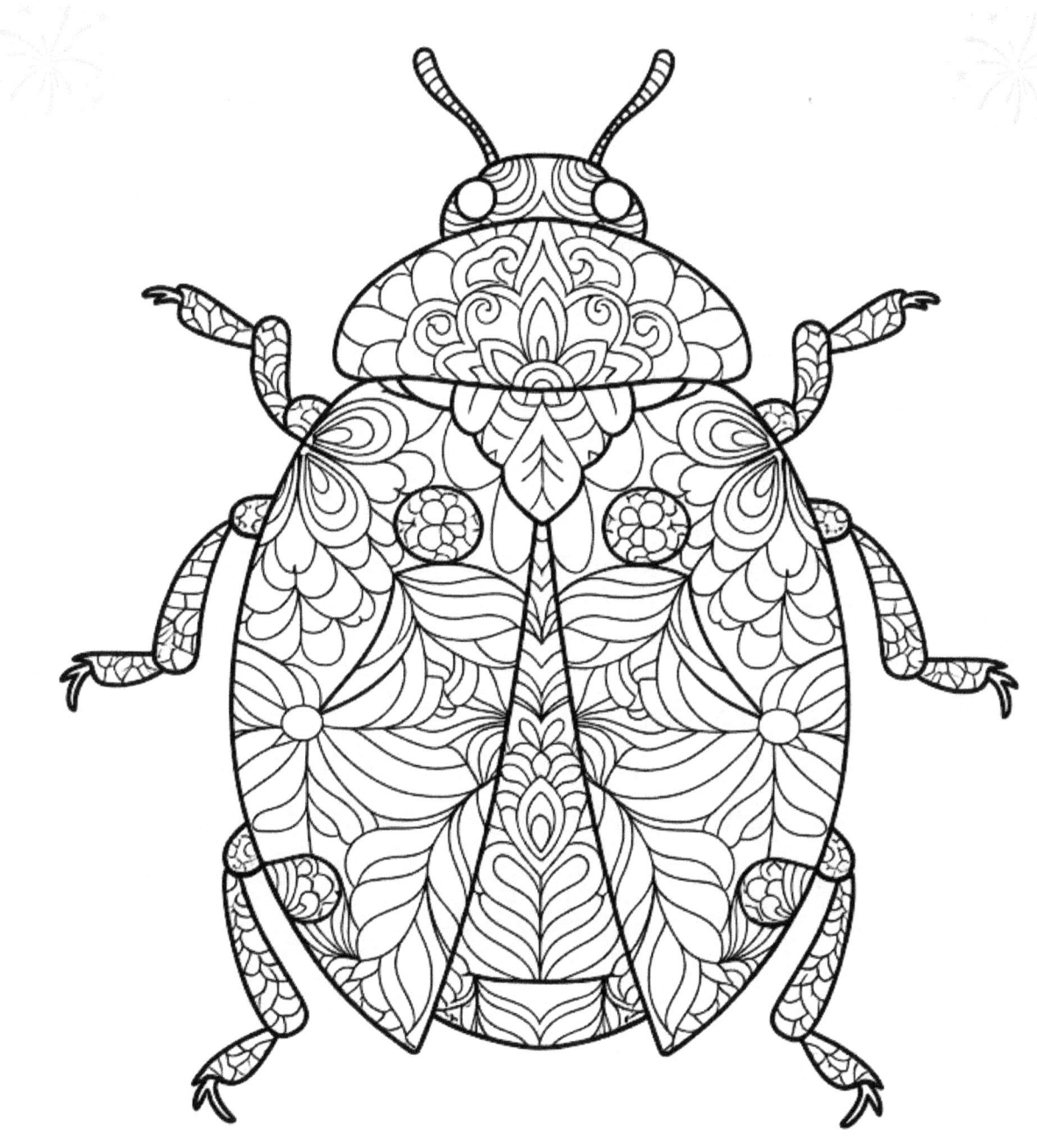

GLÜCKSKÄFER

🇹🇷 TURKEY 🇹🇷
POMEGRANATE SMASHING

Across Turkey, the New Year begins with a burst of bright red as families smash a pomegranate at their doorstep. The fruit's many seeds symbolize abundance, so the more seeds that scatter, the more prosperity the household hopes to attract. Its vibrant color has long been associated with life, fertility, and protection from misfortune.

The ritual reflects a deeper belief in starting the year with generosity and openness. By breaking the fruit wide open, people symbolically "open" their year to blessings, good fortune, and joyful surprises. It's a noisy, colorful way to signal that luck is welcome at the door.

DID YOU KNOW?

In some regions, the fruit is also hung outside the home during the year to guard against envy and bring harmony.

SMASH THE POMEGRANATE!

ECUADOR
BURNING "AÑO VIEJO" EFFIGIES

Across Turkey, the New Year begins with a burst of bright red as families smash a pomegranate at their doorstep. The fruit's many seeds symbolize abundance, so the more seeds that scatter, the more prosperity the household hopes to attract. Its vibrant color has long been associated with life, fertility, and protection from misfortune.

The ritual reflects a deeper belief in starting the year with generosity and openness. By breaking the fruit wide open, people symbolically "open" their year to blessings, good fortune, and joyful surprises. It's a noisy, colorful way to signal that luck is welcome at the door.

DID YOU KNOW?

In some regions, the fruit is also hung outside the home during the year to guard against envy and bring harmony.

ROMANIA BEAR DANCES

In parts of Romania, winter wouldn't feel complete without the famous Bear Dance. Performers don heavy fur costumes—traditionally real bear hides—and parade through villages accompanied by drummers and musicians. In Romanian folklore, bears are powerful guardians against evil, and their appearance during the darkest time of year symbolizes protection, renewal, and the coming of spring. The "bear's" movements often reenact death and rebirth, reflecting the turning of the year.

Whole communities participate in festivals where the dancers stomp, sway, and roar dramatically. The sight of dozens of "bears" moving in unison creates an unforgettable scene, blending ancient beliefs with celebratory energy. The ritual helps people let go of the previous year's hardships and step confidently into the future.

DID YOU KNOW?

Some Romanian regions claim the tradition is over 2,000 years old, rooted in ancient Dacian bear-worship practices.

AÑO VIEJO

ROMANIA BEAR DANCES

In parts of Romania, winter wouldn't feel complete without the famous Bear Dance. Performers don heavy fur costumes —traditionally real bear hides—and parade through villages accompanied by drummers and musicians. In Romanian folklore, bears are powerful guardians against evil, and their appearance during the darkest time of year symbolizes protection, renewal, and the coming of spring. The "bear's" movements often reenact death and rebirth, reflecting the turning of the year.

Whole communities participate in festivals where the dancers stomp, sway, and roar dramatically. The sight of dozens of "bears" moving in unison creates an unforgettable scene, blending ancient beliefs with celebratory energy. The ritual helps people let go of the previous year's hardships and step confidently into the future.

DID YOU KNOW?

Some Romanian regions claim the tradition is over 2,000 years old, rooted in ancient Dacian bear-worship practices.

THE BEAR DANCE

🇩🇰 DENMARK 🇩🇰
SMASHING PLATES ON DOORSTEPS

In Denmark, the New Year begins not with silence, but with a delightful crash. Friends save unused or old plates throughout the year and then break them on each other's doorsteps at midnight. The tradition is meant to wish the household good luck and strong friendships. The bigger the pile, the more loved and supported you are considered to be—making it one of Europe's most charming (and noisy) New Year customs.

The act of breaking dishes also symbolizes letting go of old troubles. By shattering the past year's frustrations, participants step into the new year with a clean slate. It's a joyful reminder that community care—and a little chaos—can bring warmth to even the coldest winter night.

DID YOU KNOW?

In some regions, people throw not just plates but also cracked cups and old bowls!

MIDNIGHT PLATE SMASH

🇺🇸 UNITED STATES 🇺🇸
TIMES SQUARE BALL DROP

Every year, millions watch the glowing New Year's Eve ball descend in New York City's Times Square. The tradition began in 1907 as a modern "time marker," replacing fireworks displays that officials considered too dangerous. The sparkling descent counts down the final seconds of the year, uniting people across the country in one shared moment.

The ball itself has evolved from a simple wood-and-iron sphere to a dazzling crystal globe illuminated by thousands of LED lights. The drop symbolizes letting go of the old year and welcoming the new with collective hope. It's not just a countdown—it's the United States' most iconic ritual of renewal.

DID YOU KNOW?

The Times Square ball weighs nearly 12,000 pounds and stays on display year-round.

THE BALL DROP

COLOMBIA
SWEEPING THE HOUSE AT 12AM

In Colombia, a midnight sweep isn't just good housekeeping—it's a powerful symbol. Families sweep the floors right at the year's turning point to push out bad energy, lingering misfortune, and any negativity clinging to the old year. The direction matters too: sweeping toward the door sends troubles outward, making space for good luck to flow in.

The practice comes from a blend of cultural and spiritual beliefs that connect cleanliness with renewal. By tidying the home at such a symbolic moment, Colombians reaffirm a desire for clarity, peace, and fresh beginnings. It's a simple act with meaningful emotional weight.

DID YOU KNOW?

Some households pair sweeping with opening all the windows and doors at midnight—letting the old year out and the new one in.

SWEEP OUT THE OLD YEAR

JAPAN
LUCKY FOX MASKS (KITSUNE)

Kitsune masks are worn during festivals and celebrations connected to Inari, the Shinto deity of rice, prosperity, and good harvests. Foxes are believed to be Inari's messengers, moving between the human and spiritual worlds. Wearing a kitsune mask at New Year is thought to invite the fox's cleverness, protection, and blessing, especially during times of transition when guidance is most needed.

These masks also appear in dances, parades, and shrine visits, where their playful expressions symbolize transformation and new beginnings. In many communities, a fox mask serves as a reminder that luck can come from unexpected places and that the new year is a chance to change, grow, or reinvent oneself—just as Kitsune are said to shapeshift in legends.

DID YOU KNOW?

In some regions, families leave offerings of fried tofu—Inari's favorite food—at shrines to attract good fortune for the coming year.

KITSUNE

🇵🇪 PERU 🇵🇪
RUNNING AROUND THE BLOCK WITH A SUITCASE

In Peru, travel lovers have a special New Year's trick: grab an empty suitcase and run around the block at the stroke of midnight. According to tradition, the speed and enthusiasm of your suitcase sprint help determine how much travel you'll enjoy in the coming year. Whether you hope for a tropical vacation, a family visit, or a grand adventure, this quirky ritual turns the desire to explore into a joyful midnight dash.

The custom is often shared with laughter, neighbors cheering one another on as the new year begins. Some households circle the house instead of the entire block, keeping the spirit of the ritual even in small spaces. It's a lighthearted reminder to start the year with motion and optimism.

DID YOU KNOW?

Variations of the suitcase run appear in Colombia, Ecuador, and Venezuela—proof that wanderlust is truly contagious.

SUITCASE RUN!

IRELAND
HITTING THE WALLS WITH BREAD

An old Irish New Year's custom involves taking a loaf of bread —traditionally a round soda bread—and lightly striking it against the walls of the home. This unusual ritual was believed to chase away evil spirits, hunger, or misfortune that might linger from the year before. The bread, as a symbol of nourishment, was thought to bless the household with plenty for the year ahead.

While fewer people practice it today, the tradition lives on in stories and folklore, reminding families of Ireland's long history of symbolic food rituals. It transforms the simple act of baking and sharing bread into a wish for stability and abundance.

DID YOU KNOW?

In some regions, after "banishing" the spirits, families would enjoy the same loaf as part of their New Year's breakfast.

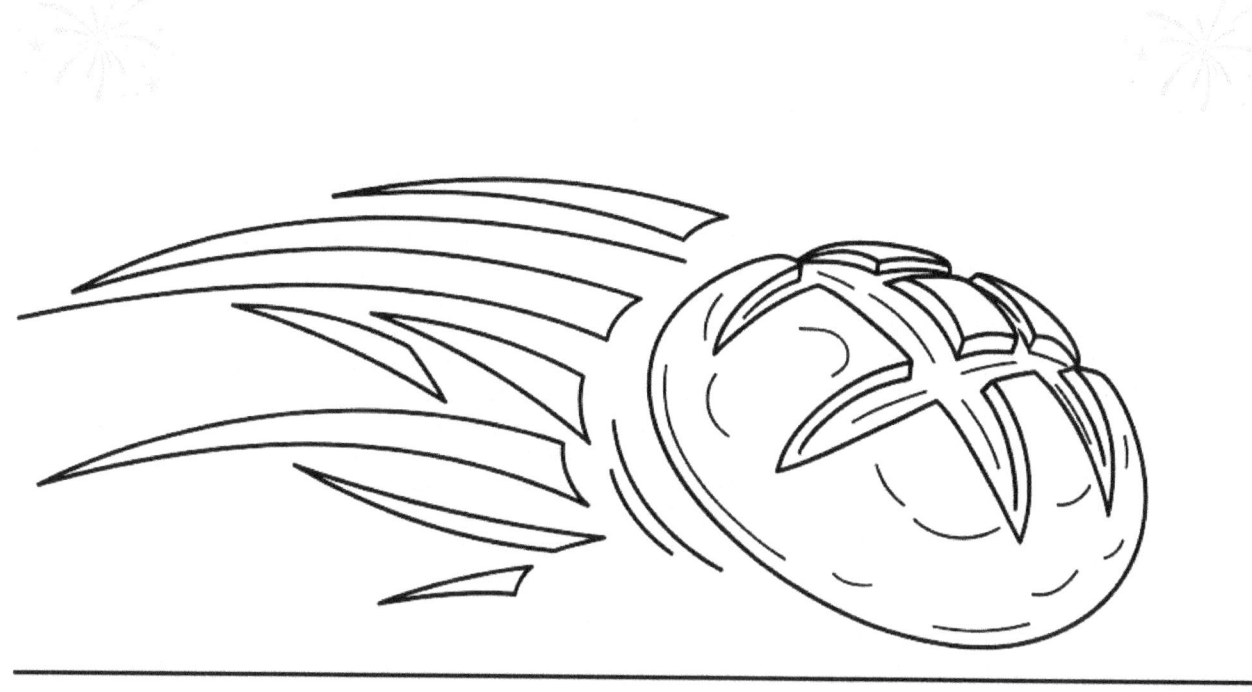

BREAD FOR BLESSINGS

✚ FINLAND ✚
NEW YEAR TIN CASTING

In Finland, New Year's Eve brings a beloved fortune-telling ritual called tin casting, or uudenvuodentina. Small pieces of tin (traditionally lead-tin alloy horseshoes) are melted over a flame until liquid. The molten tin is then poured quickly into a bowl of cold water, where it hardens into a surprising shape. The resulting sculpture is examined for clues: a heart might suggest romance, a ship could mean travel, and a flower might promise happiness.

Families and friends gather to compare their tin figures and share predictions for the year ahead. The interpretations can be serious or silly, but the ritual is always magical—part craft, part mystery, and part shared laughter as everyone guesses what the future may hold.

DID YOU KNOW?

In recent years, Finland has replaced lead-based casting tins with eco-friendly alternatives to keep the tradition safe and modern.

UUDENVUODENTINA

UKRAINE
DID MOROZ

Father Frost is a beloved winter figure across Eastern Slavic cultures. Unlike Santa Claus, he is not tied to Christmas alone—he rules the entire winter season, bringing blessings, protection, and a bit of icy magic. Traditionally, he travels through forests with his granddaughter, Snegurochka (the Snow Maiden), delivering gifts and guarding homes from the hardships of winter.

His presence in New Year celebrations reflects older folklore about winter spirits who guided people through the darkest months. Father Frost represents strength, endurance, and the return of light after long cold nights. Invoking his protection is a way of welcoming warmth, luck, and renewal for the year ahead.

DID YOU KNOW?

In some regions, children must sing a poem or dance before Father Frost will present them with gifts.

DID MOROZ

 PORTUGAL
JUMPING INTO THE OCEAN

On Portugal's coasts, the bravest celebrants greet the New Year with a freezing plunge into the Atlantic. This brisk ritual symbolizes washing away the old year's troubles and stepping into a fresh beginning with courage and clarity. Even on chilly winter mornings, crowds gather on beaches to leap into the waves together.

For many, the dip is as much spiritual as it is physical: the shock of cold water is believed to "reset" the mind and body, cleansing away misfortune. The shared experience also strengthens community bonds—starting the year united, invigorated, and full of hope.

DID YOU KNOW?

Some participants jump exactly seven waves, a number tied to good luck and ancient sea myths in Portuguese folklore.

SEVEN WAVES

GERMANY
LUCKY FOX MASKS (KITSUNE)

For centuries in Germany, running into a chimney sweep on New Year's Day was considered one of the luckiest moments of the year. Sweeps were traditionally associated with clearing away soot and fire hazards, which symbolically translated into clearing away misfortune. Their black uniforms and tools came to represent protection, hard work, and a fresh start.

Today, chimney sweeps still appear in holiday markets and local celebrations, offering good-luck charms shaped like tiny sweeps or sweeping brushes. Spotting one on January 1st—or receiving a charm—remains a cheerful wish for prosperity and safety in the coming year.

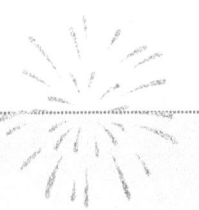

DID YOU KNOW?

The German phrase "Schornsteinfeger bringen Glück" literally means "chimney sweeps bring luck."

SCHORNSTEINFEGER

RUSSIA
LUCKY FOX MASKS (KITSUNE)

In Russia, some New Year's Eve celebrations include a dramatic little ritual for luck and intention-setting. People write a short wish on a small piece of paper, light it on fire just before midnight, and let the ashes fall into a glass of champagne. If you drink the champagne before the last bell tolls, tradition says your wish has a higher chance of coming true.

This tiny ceremony blends symbolism with a sense of fun: fire transforms the wish, the ashes represent acceptance, and the champagne carries the intention into the new year. Friends often join in, making the moment both personal and festive.

DID YOU KNOW?

The ritual must be completed—burn, drop, and drink—within one minute for the superstition to "work," adding a playful element of speed and suspense.

BURN, DROP, WISH!

JAPAN
JOYA NO KANE (108 BELL RINGS)

Across Japan, Buddhist temples ring their great bronze bells exactly 108 times on New Year's Eve—a ritual called Joya no Kane. The number 108 represents the human temptations or "earthly desires" that cause suffering according to Buddhist teaching. As the deep, resonant bell echoes through the night, each strike symbolically clears away one of these burdens, helping people enter the new year with a purified mind and an unweighted heart.

Many temples invite visitors to take a turn ringing the bell themselves, often lining up around the grounds as the final minutes of the year slip away. The slow, rhythmic tolls create a calming soundtrack to midnight, turning the transition between years into a moment of collective reflection, hope, and renewal.

DID YOU KNOW?

Some temples begin ringing earlier in the evening so the final strike aligns perfectly with midnight—ending the year on a single, cleansing note.

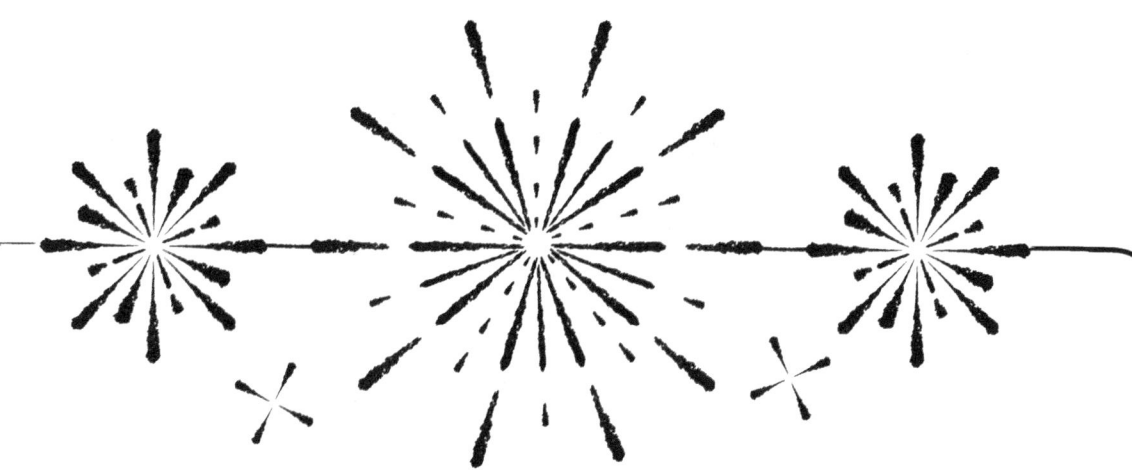

FOODS & FLAVORS OF GOOD FORTUNE

Across the world, many New Year traditions begin at the table. The foods people cook, share, and savor are more than meals—they're symbols of hope. Whether it's noodles for long life, lentils for wealth, grapes for good luck, or dishes shared in the spirit of abundance, each recipe carries a wish for the year ahead. In this section, you'll explore how global cultures use flavor, color, and creativity to turn ordinary ingredients into powerful good-luck charms.

HAPPY NEW YEAR

PHILIPPINES
12 ROUND FRUITS

In Filipino households, New Year's Eve tables are filled with twelve round fruits, each one representing good fortune for one month of the coming year. Round shapes symbolize coins, and the variety of colors and flavors creates a vibrant display meant to attract prosperity. Families carefully select fruits like oranges, grapes, apples, melons, and dragon fruit to complete their lucky dozen.

This tradition reflects a wider Filipino New Year's theme: round = wealth. Many families also wear polka dots or carry coins in their pockets to amplify the good luck.

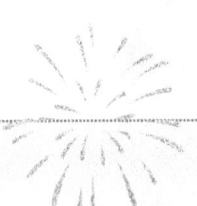

DID YOU KNOW?

Some families go beyond twelve fruits—displaying as many round fruits as possible to supercharge their luck.

12 ROUND FRUITS

 GHANA
LUCKY FOX MASKS (KITSUNE)

Jollof rice is one of West Africa's most beloved dishes, and in Ghana it plays a delicious role in New Year celebrations. The meal—rich with tomatoes, peppers, onions, and warming spices—is shared with friends and family as a symbol of plenty. Because Jollof is festive, vibrant, and served in generous portions, it naturally became tied to wishes for abundance in the year ahead. Gathering around a shared pot reflects the belief that prosperity grows when it is enjoyed together.

Across Ghana, cooking Jollof for the holidays is also a way of honoring community and home. Families often use cherished recipes passed down through generations, blending flavors that represent comfort, heritage, and hope. Beginning the year with food made from the heart sets a joyful tone for the months to come.

DID YOU KNOW?

West Africa has a playful "Jollof rivalry," with Ghana and Nigeria each claiming their version is the best.

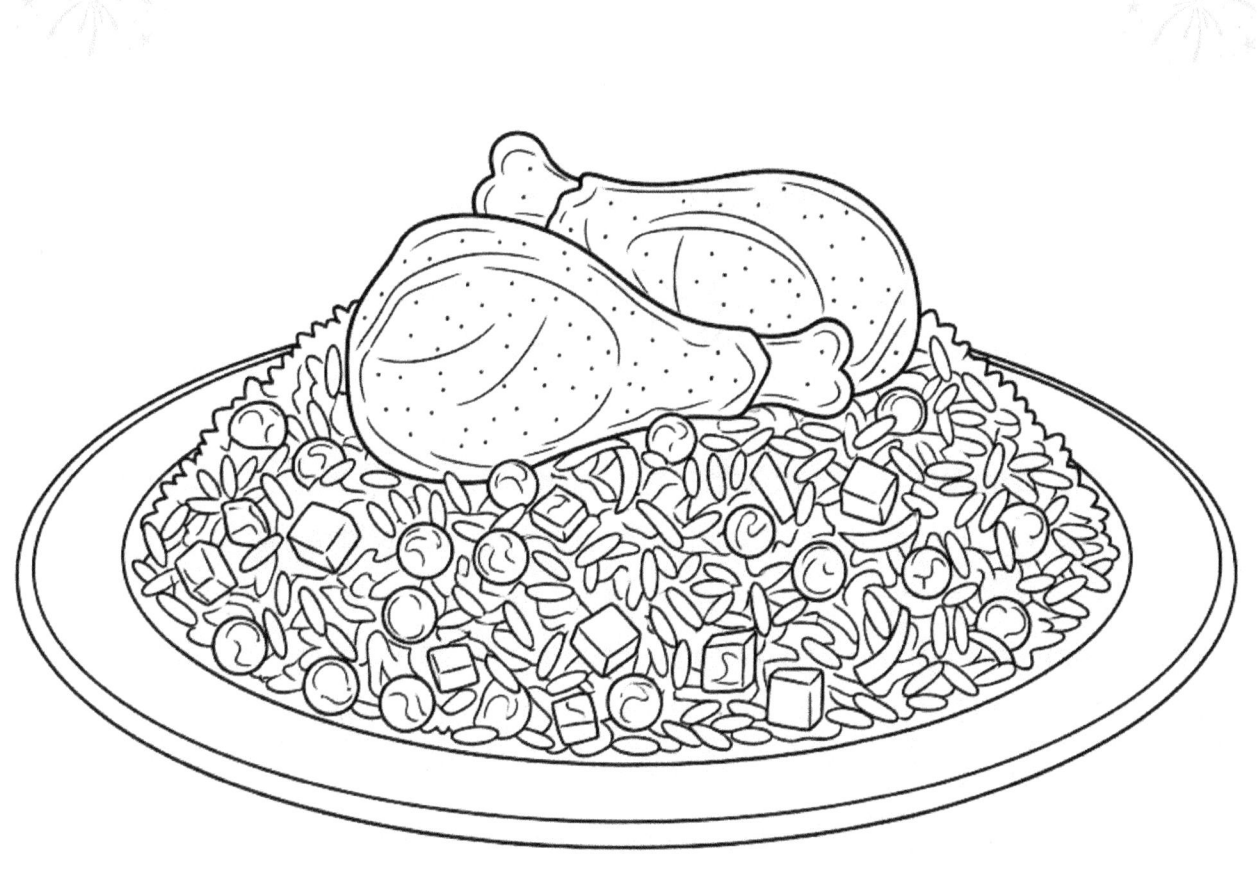

JOLLOF!

JAPAN

TOSHIKOSHI SOBA ("YEAR-CROSSING NOODLES")

On New Year's Eve in Japan, families eat a warm bowl of soba noodles to "cross over" from the old year into the new. The noodles are long, symbolizing long life, and easy to cut with chopsticks—representing the gentle release of last year's hardships. The tradition is calming and reflective, offering a moment of quiet before the fireworks, shrine visits, and celebrations begin.

Different regions prepare the dish in unique ways, but the meaning stays the same: a wish for health, resilience, and a smooth transition into the year ahead. Many people say that finishing the bowl ensures extra good luck.

DID YOU KNOW?

Soba is made from buckwheat, a plant known for surviving tough weather—making it a symbol of strength and endurance in Japanese culture.

TOSHIKOSHI SOBA
年越しそば

ITALY
LENTILS FOR GOOD FORTUNE

In Italy, the first meal of the New Year often includes lentils—tiny round legumes that resemble coins. Eating them on New Year's Eve is believed to bring wealth and prosperity in the months ahead. The dish is hearty, comforting, and usually paired with slices of cotechino sausage, which symbolizes abundance.

The tradition dates back to the Roman Empire, when people would give small pouches of lentils as gifts, hoping they would "turn into money" as the year unfolded. Today, families across Italy still enjoy steaming bowls of lentils as the clock strikes midnight, sending a warm and hopeful message to the year to come.

DID YOU KNOW?

The more lentils you eat on New Year's, the more wealth you're supposed to receive—so some Italians make sure their bowls are very full!

LENTILS FOR LUCK

SPAIN
THE 12 GRAPES AT MIDNIGHT

In Spain, the New Year countdown comes with a twist: at each of the 12 bell strikes, people eat one grape—each symbolizing a lucky month ahead. This joyful, slightly frantic tradition began in the late 1800s and quickly became beloved nationwide. Town squares, living rooms, and television audiences all join in as the clock chimes, racing to finish their grapes before the final bell.

The tradition has spread far beyond Spain, appearing in many Spanish-speaking communities worldwide. Whether the grapes bring good luck or not, they definitely bring laughter, excitement, and a fun challenge to the New Year celebration.

DID YOU KNOW?

Some people peel and seed their grapes beforehand so they don't choke or fall behind during the lightning-fast 12-second countdown!

12 LUCKY GRAPES

 MOROCCO
SEVEN-VEGETABLE COUSCOUS

In Morocco and across Amazigh communities, couscous is far more than a meal—it's a centerpiece of celebration. For the Amazigh New Year (Yennayer), families prepare couscous with seven vegetables, a number believed to carry good fortune. Each vegetable symbolizes blessings such as health, growth, and prosperity. The dish honors the agricultural roots of Amazigh culture and welcomes a year filled with nourishment and balance.

Sharing couscous on this day also connects generations, as the tradition is rooted in seasonal cycles and gratitude for the harvest. Preparing it together—washing vegetables, steaming grains, gathering at a communal table—turns the meal into a ritual of unity and renewal.

DID YOU KNOW?

Some families add seven spices as well, doubling the "lucky seven" symbolism.

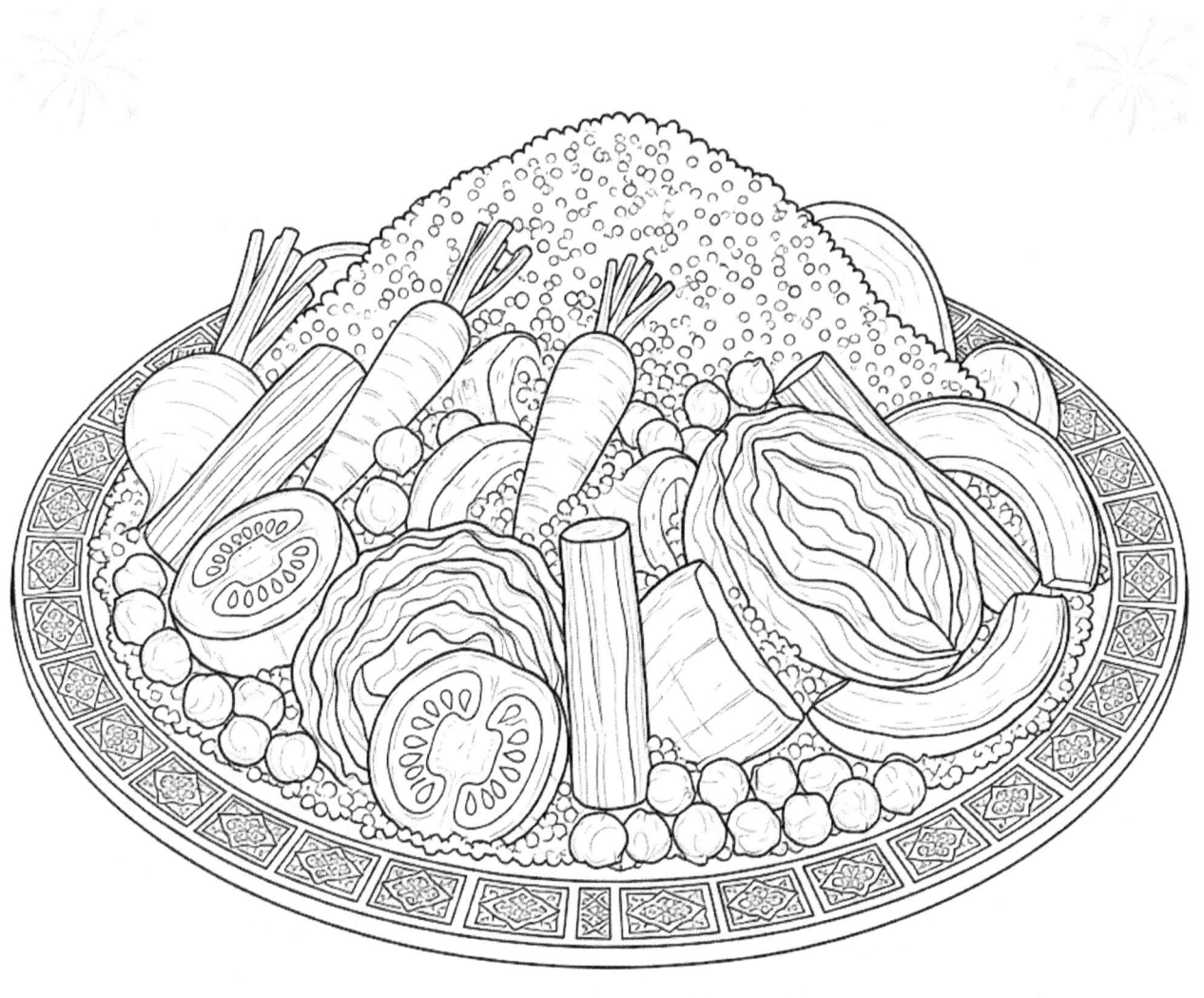

كسكس بالسبع خضاري

KSEKSU B-SBAʿ KHDARI

🇩🇰 DENMARK 🇩🇰
KRANSEKAGE TOWER CAKE

Kransekage, a ring-shaped almond cake stacked into a tall tower, is a festive centerpiece in Denmark's New Year celebrations. Each ring symbolizes unity and continuity, making the towering cake a sweet expression of connection and hope for the year ahead. Its crunchy exterior and chewy interior make it a beloved treat for weddings, holidays, and especially New Year's Eve.

Families often break off pieces together at midnight, marking a shared step into the coming year. Its circular shape echoes the idea of cycles—endings becoming beginnings, and communities holding together.

DID YOU KNOW?

Despite being called a "cake," kransekage is closer to a chewy almond pastry and is often decorated with icing swirls or tiny Danish flags.

KRANSEKAGE

 USA
BLACK-EYED PEAS & COLLARD GREENS

In many parts of the American South, New Year's Day isn't complete without a plate of black-eyed peas and collard greens. The peas symbolize coins, representing luck and financial opportunity, while the greens resemble folded paper money. Together, the meal becomes a tasty wish for abundance and prosperity in the months ahead.

The tradition has roots in African, Indigenous, and Southern foodways, blending cultural memory with hopes for survival and renewal. For many families, this New Year's dish is not just symbolic—it's a comforting ritual shared across generations.

DID YOU KNOW?

In some regions, families leave offerings of fried tofu—Inari's favorite food—at shrines to attract good fortune for the coming year.

LUCKY PEAS & GREENS

GREECE
VASILOPITA CAKE

Vasilopita is a special New Year's cake served in Greek homes on January 1st in honor of St. Basil the Great, one of early Christianity's most beloved saints. St. Basil is remembered for his generosity to the poor, and legend tells of him distributing coins to families in need. To commemorate that spirit of charity and blessing, a shiny coin is hidden inside the cake batter before baking. When the cake is sliced—one piece for each family member—the person who finds the coin is believed to receive a year of good luck, protection, and opportunity.

More than a dessert, Vasilopita is a ritual of sharing, anticipation, and family unity. Each slice represents hope for the coming months, and the ceremony of cutting the cake is often a centerpiece of New Year gatherings. Whether sweet and cake-like or bread-like and braided, it reflects regional customs and cherished family recipes.

DID YOU KNOW?

In many Greek homes, the very first slice is cut "for Jesus," a tradition dating back centuries and rooted in Christian hospitality.

VASILOPITA

GERMANY
MARZIPAN PIGS
(GLÜCKSSCHWEIN)

In Germany, marzipan pigs—called Glücksschwein, or "lucky pigs"—are given as sweet gifts for the New Year. Pigs have long symbolized prosperity, strength, and good fortune in German folklore, and receiving one means someone is wishing you a year filled with success and abundance. These tiny treats come shaped as smiling pink pigs and are often exchanged among friends, classmates, and coworkers.

The pig's association with luck dates back to medieval times, when owning pigs meant your household would not go hungry. Over time, the sturdy animal became a cheerful emblem of perseverance, comfort, and well-being.

DID YOU KNOW?

The phrase Schwein haben in German literally means "to have a pig"—but idiomatically it means "to be lucky."

GLÜCKSSCHWEIN

NATURE, LIGHT & THE SPIRIT OF RENEWAL

From the first sunrise in New Zealand to the blooming Meskel daisies of Ethiopia, many New Year traditions are rooted in the natural world. These celebrations honor the changing seasons, the return of light, and our deep connection to land and sky. In this section, you'll meet figures like Father Frost and symbols like the upstream-swimming carp—reminders that nature itself guides the rhythms of hope, endurance, and renewal. Together, these traditions show how the New Year can be a moment of harmony with the world around us.

HAPPY NEW YEAR

 ALL OVER THE WORLD FIREWORKS!

For centuries, fireworks have lit up the sky to mark the turning of the year. The tradition began in ancient China, where loud explosions and bright flashes were believed to scare away wandering spirits before the new year arrived. As gunpowder technology spread across the world, so did the dramatic practice of greeting midnight with light and sound. Today, fireworks are a global symbol of celebration, excitement, and hopeful beginnings.

Modern New Year fireworks are more than just a show; they represent the wish to start the year boldly and brightly. From Sydney's harbor to Rio's beaches to New York's skyline, millions watch the skies erupt in color, joining in one shared moment of awe as the old year fades and the new one bursts into view.

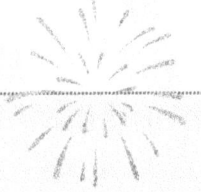

DID YOU KNOW?

The first "firecrackers" weren't gunpowder at all. Ancient Chinese people burned bamboo, which popped loudly when heated thanks to the air pockets inside!

ETHIOPIA
ENKUTATASH
(SEPTEMBER NEW YEAR)

Ethiopia's New Year, Enkutatash, is celebrated in September, when the rainy season ends and the countryside bursts into bright yellow Meskel daisies. The blooming landscape symbolizes renewal, hope, and the start of a fresh agricultural year. Families wear traditional white clothing, share festive meals, and exchange cards and flowers as blessings for the months ahead.

Unlike the cold winter New Year familiar in many countries, Enkutatash marks a spring-like moment of rebirth. Children sing songs and visit neighbors with bundles of daisies, while community gatherings highlight gratitude and joy. The celebration reflects Ethiopia's unique calendar and deep connection to seasonal cycles.

DID YOU KNOW?

Ethiopia follows its own calendar, which is about seven to eight years "behind" the widely used Gregorian calendar.

ENKUTATASH

CHINA
CARP SWIMMING UPSTREAM

In China, the image of a carp swimming upstream comes from an ancient legend: a determined carp fought its way up a powerful river and, upon leaping over the mythical "Dragon Gate," transformed into a dragon. This story symbolizes perseverance, ambition, and the triumph that comes from steady effort. During New Year celebrations, the carp becomes a wish for progress, strength, and success in school, career, or personal goals.

Carp (usually represented as koi) appear in New Year art, decorations, and gift-giving because they embody the spirit of overcoming obstacles. Their upward movement mirrors the hope that the coming year will bring growth—both through hard work and through embracing challenges as stepping stones.

DID YOU KNOW?

The phrase "carp leaping over the Dragon Gate" is still used today to congratulate students who pass major exams or people who achieve big milestones.

CARP DRAGON GATE
鲤鱼跃龙门

🇳🇿 NEW ZEALAND 🇳🇿
FIRST SUNRISE OF THE YEAR

New Zealand is one of the first places on Earth to see the new day, which makes watching the year's first sunrise especially meaningful. Many people gather on East Coast beaches or climb spots like Mount Hikurangi to greet the sun as it rises over the Pacific. In Māori tradition, marking the first dawn connects the community to renewal, hope, and the natural rhythms that guide the year.

For families and travelers alike, standing in the early-morning glow becomes a symbol of fresh beginnings. As the sky shifts from night to blazing color, people reflect on the year behind them and set intentions for the one ahead—beginning the new year literally "in the light."

DID YOU KNOW?

Mount Hikurangi is considered the first place on the mainland to see the sunrise and holds deep cultural importance as a sacred mountain for the Ngāti Porou people.

TE RĀ O TE TAU HOU (FIRST SUNRISE)

PUZZLE: MATCHING GAME

Connect the Tradition to the Country! (Answers on page 92)

TRADITIONS **COUNTRIES**

1) Running with a suitcase at 12AM to invite travel.

A) Greece

2) Hidden coin in a New Year cake brings luck.

B) Peru

3) Smashing plates at a friend's door to bring good fortune.

C) Denmark

4) Pouring melted tin into water to reveal fortunes.

D) Spain

5) Eating 12 grapes at midnight for twelve months of luck.

E) Ethiopia

6) Smashing a pomegranate so its seeds scatter for abundance.

F) Germany

7) Marzipan pig candies given as good-luck charms.

G) Turkey

8) Hitting the walls with bread to chase out spirits and hunger.

H) Japan

9) Long soba noodles eaten to cross into the year with long life.

I) Ecuador

10) Burning an "Old Year" effigy to banish misfortune.

J) USA

11) Yellow flowers and white clothing mark a September New Year of renewal.

K) Finland

12) Round fruits displayed and eaten at midnight for prosperity.

L) Philippines

13) Lentils eaten as symbols of wealth.

M) Ireland

14) Bear costumes parading through villages to chase away winter misfortune.

N) Romania

15) Black-eyed peas and collard greens eaten for money and good fortune.

O) Italy

ACTIVITY
12 GRAPES, 12 TWELVE WISHES FOR THE NEW YEAR

Origins: The tradition originates from Spain, dating back to at least the 1890s. There are a few theories about how it started: one suggests grape growers launched a marketing campaign to sell surplus grapes by associating them with wishes and good luck, while another claims wealthy Spaniards in the 1880s were imitating French bourgeoisie celebrations.

Where it's practiced: The tradition is widespread throughout Spanish-speaking communities, particularly in Spain, Mexico, Guatemala, El Salvador, and other Central and Latin American countries. It began as an upper-class practice that eventually spread throughout society.

How it works: You eat one grape with each of the 12 midnight chimes, making a wish with each grape for the corresponding month of the coming year. Some families even write down their wishes on paper as they eat each grape.

WHAT 12 THINGS DO YOU WISH FOR THIS YEAR?
Use each of the following pages to visualize and outline each one!

1: MY FIRST WISH FOR THE NEW YEAR

2: MY SECOND WISH FOR THE NEW YEAR

3: MY THIRD WISH FOR THE NEW YEAR

4: MY FOURTH WISH FOR THE NEW YEAR

5: MY FIFTH WISH FOR THE NEW YEAR

6: MY SIXTH WISH FOR THE NEW YEAR

7: MY SEVENTH WISH FOR THE NEW YEAR

8: MY EIGHTH WISH FOR THE NEW YEAR

9: MY NINTH WISH FOR THE NEW YEAR

10: MY TENTH WISH FOR THE NEW YEAR

11: MY ELEVENTH WISH FOR THE NEW YEAR

12: MY TWELFTH WISH FOR THE NEW YEAR

HAPPY NEW YEAR

Festive greetings from every corner of the globe.

🇨🇳 CHINA
新年快乐 (XĪNNIÁN KUÀILÈ)
(MANDARIN: "HAPPY NEW YEAR")
PRONUNCIATION: SHEEN-NYEN KWAI-LUH

🇨🇴 COLOMBIA
FELIZ AÑO NUEVO
(SPANISH: "HAPPY NEW YEAR")
PRONUNCIATION: FEH-LEES AH-NYO NWEH-VO

🇩🇰 DENMARK
GODT NYTÅR
(DANISH: "HAPPY NEW YEAR")
PRONUNCIATION: GOT NEU-DOR

🇪🇨 ECUADOR
FELIZ AÑO NUEVO
(SPANISH: "HAPPY NEW YEAR")
PRONUNCIATION: FEH-LEES AH-NYO NWEH-VO

🇪🇹 ETHIOPIA
MELKAM ADDIS AMET
(AMHARIC: "HAPPY NEW YEAR")
PRONUNCIATION: MEL-KAM AH-DIS AH-MET

🇫🇮 FINLAND
HYVÄÄ UUTTA VUOTTA
(FINNISH: "HAPPY NEW YEAR")
PRONUNCIATION: HÜ-VAH OO-TAH VUO-TAH

🇩🇪 GERMANY
FROHES NEUES JAHR
(GERMAN: "HAPPY NEW YEAR")
PRONUNCIATION: FRO-ESS NOY-ESS YAR

🇬🇭 GHANA
AFEHYIA PA
(AKAN/TWI: "GOOD YEAR MEETING")
PRONUNCIATION: AH-FEH-HYEE-AH PAH

HAPPY NEW YEAR

Festive greetings from every corner of the globe.

🇬🇷 GREECE
Καλή Χρονιά **(KALÍ CHRONIÁ)**
(GREEK: "GOOD YEAR")
PRONUNCIATION: KAH-LEE CHROH-NYAH

🇮🇪 IRELAND
ATHBHLIAIN FAOI MHAISE DHUIT
(IRISH GAELIC: "HAPPY NEW YEAR")
PRONUNCIATION: AH-VLEEN FWEE WAH-SHA GHITCH

🇮🇹 ITALY
FELICE ANNO NUOVO
(ITALIAN: "HAPPY NEW YEAR")
PRONUNCIATION: FEH-LEE-CHEH AHN-NO NWOH-VO

🇯🇵 JAPAN
明けましておめでとうございます
(AKEMASHITE OMEDETŌ GOZAIMASU)
(JAPANESE: "HAPPY NEW YEAR")
PRONUNCIATION: AH-KEH-MAH-SHTEH OH-MEH-DEH-TOH GOH-ZAH-EE-MAS

🇲🇦 MOROCCO
BONNE ANNÉE
(FRENCH: "HAPPY NEW YEAR")
PRONUNCIATION: BON AH-NAY

سنة سعيدة **(SANA SAIDA)**
(MOROCCAN ARABIC, DARIJA: "HAPPY NEW YEAR")
PRONUNCIATION: SAH-NAH SAH-EE-DAH

HAPPY NEW YEAR

Festive greetings from every corner of the globe.

🇳🇿 NEW ZEALAND
HARI TAU HOU
(MāORI: "HAPPY NEW YEAR")
PRONUNCIATION: HAH-REE TOE-HO

🇵🇪 PERU
FELIZ AÑO NUEVO
(SPANISH: "HAPPY NEW YEAR")
PRONUNCIATION: FEH-LEES AH-NYO NWEH-VO

🇵🇭 PHILIPPINES
MANIGONG BAGONG TAON
(FILIPINO/TAGALOG: "HAPPY NEW YEAR")
PRONUNCIATION: MAH-NEE-GONG BAH-GONG TAH-ON

🇵🇹 PORTUGAL
FELIZ AÑO NUEVO
(SPANISH: "HAPPY NEW YEAR")
PRONUNCIATION: FEH-LEES AH-NYO NWEH-VO

🇷🇴 ROMANIA
LA MULȚI ANI
(ROMANIAN: "TO MANY YEARS!")
PRONUNCIATION: LAH MOOL-TSEE AHN

🇷🇺 RUSSIA
С Новым Годом (S NOVYM GODOM)
(RUSSIAN: "HAPPY NEW YEAR")
PRONUNCIATION: S NO-VIM GO-DUM

🇪🇸 SPAIN
FELIZ AÑO NUEVO
(SPANISH: "HAPPY NEW YEAR")
PRONUNCIATION: FEH-LEES AH-NYO NWEH-VO

🇹🇷 TURKEY
(TURKISH: "HAPPY NEW YEAR")
PRONUNCIATION: MOOT-LOO YIL-LAR

HAPPY NEW YEAR

Festive greetings from every corner of the globe.

🇺🇦 UKRAINE
З Новим Роком **(Z NOVYM ROKOM)**
(UKRAINIAN: "HAPPY NEW YEAR")
PRONUNCIATION: Z NO-VYM RO-KUM

🇺🇸 USA
HAPPY NEW YEAR!
(ENGLISH)

Also from Pettyfeather Publishing

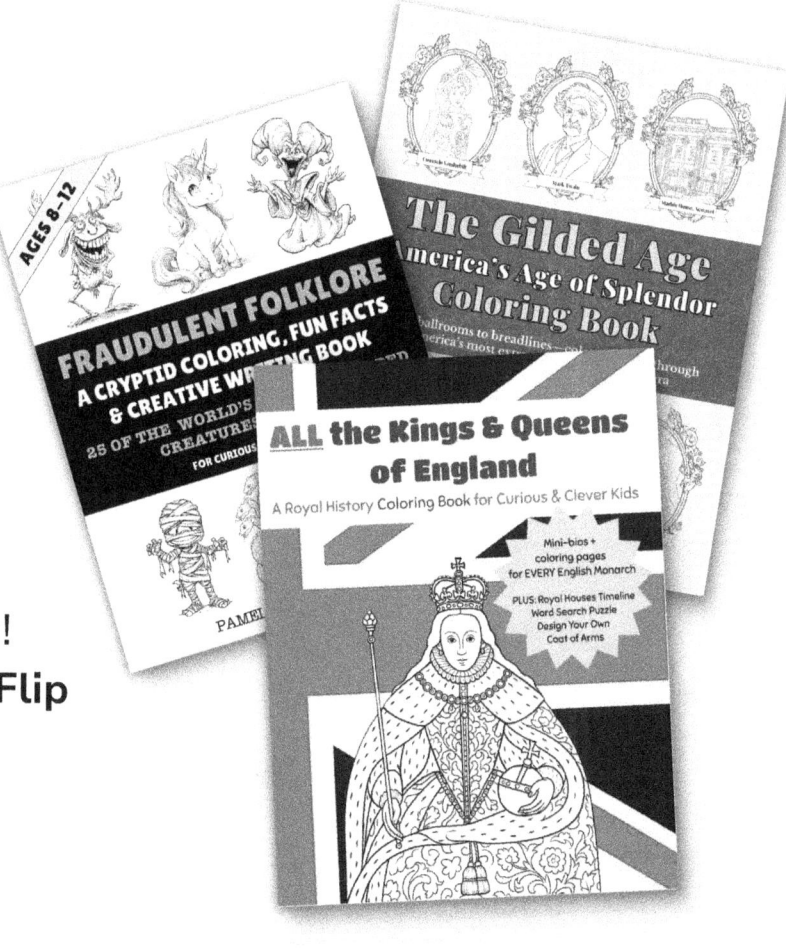

EDUCATIONAL COLORING BOOKS

Books that pair short articles, activities and coloring pages for kids ages 8-12 to make learning more fun and coloring more enriching! **Available on Amazon. Flip this page for more details.**

CHAPTER + ACTIVITY BOOKS

Global and historical explorations of holidays & events for kids ages 8-12. **Available on Amazon. Scan the QR code to learn more!**

COLOR 1,000+ YEARS OF ENGLISH ROYAL HISTORY!

"A fantastic way to introduce kids to English history! Informative, well-designed, and fun to explore!"

— Amazon UK Reviewer

55 Monarchs

Tons of Fun Facts

One epic coloring adventure!

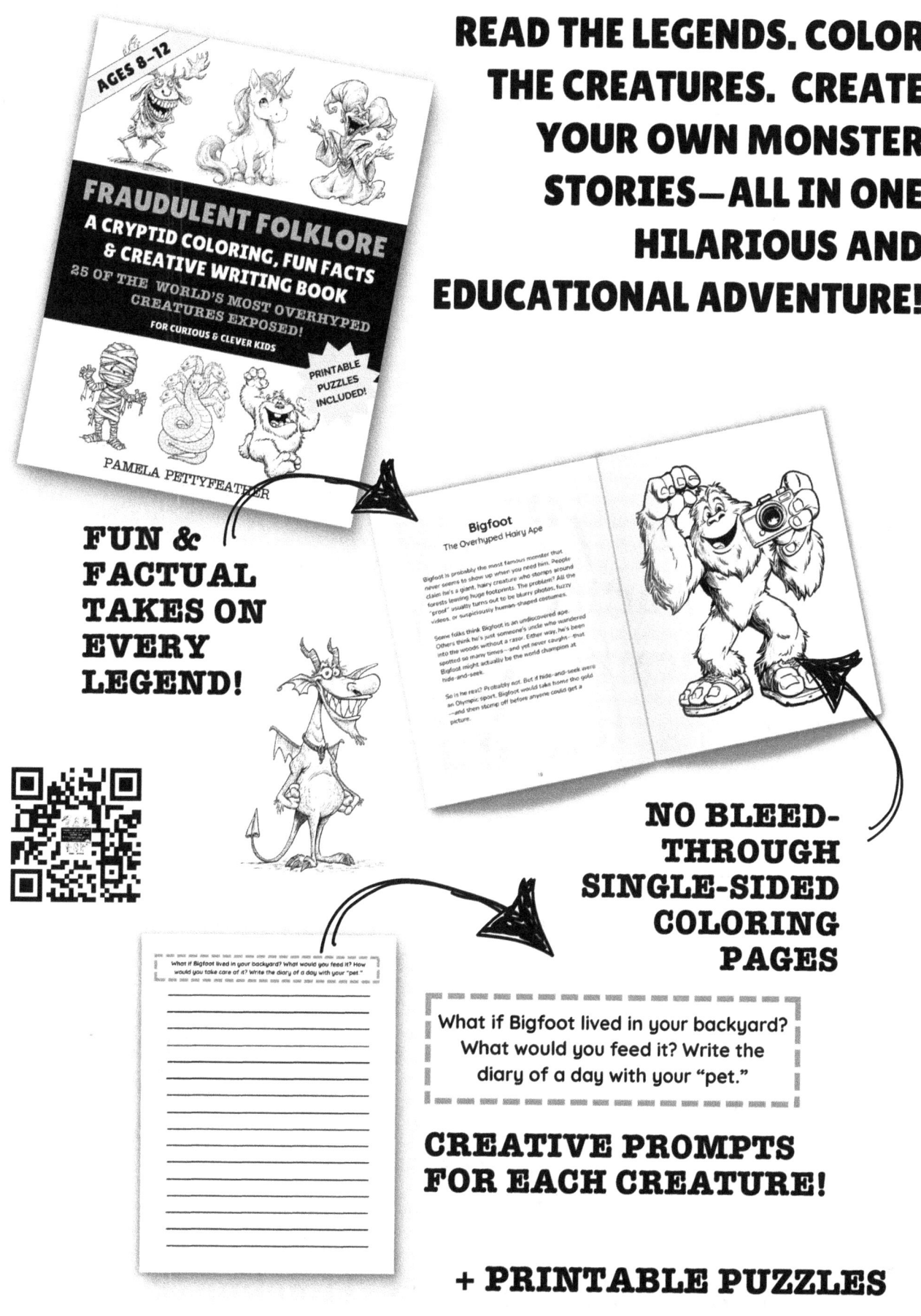

COLOR THE DRAMA, ELEGANCE & WONDER OF A DAZZLING ERA.

Coloring pages drawn from historic photographs, cartoons & paintings

Witty, 1-page educational articles to contemplate while coloring

Plus: A Gilded Age Glossary, Timeline & Games!

MEET THE PRESIDENTS OF THE UNITED STATES!

Color 250 Years of AMERICAN History!

Kid-Friendly Bios, Fun Facts & Coloring Pages for Each President

If I Were President... Activity Invites kids to envision themselves as president and outline their agenda

Plus: Easy-to-understand overviews of major eras of American history

JOIN OUR MAILING LIST

for bonus printable coloring pages & fun fact sheets and for news about our next Educational Coloring Books!

MATCHING GAME ANSWERS

1 → B (Peru)
2 → A (Greece)
3 → C (Denmark)
4 → K (Finland)
5 → D (Spain)
6 → G (Turkey)
7 → F (Germany)
8 → M (Ireland)
9 → H (Japan)
10 → I (Ecuador)
11 → E (Ethiopia)
12 → L (Philippines)
13 → O (Italy)
14 → N (Romania)
15 → J (United States)

www.ingramcontent.com/pod-product-compliance
Lightning Source LLC
Chambersburg PA
CBHW080551030426
42337CB00024B/4831